THE TRANSFORMATION OF THE CHURCH
"Come out of Babylon"

Includes Bonus Book
What's Wrong With The Church?

Copyright Dani'El Garvin
ISBN: 9798680665879
Do not copy without permission
Quotes are allowed as long as there is proper citation

DEDICATION

My friends
Benjamin Raven Pressley
Vinnie Holman
Elaine Sion Rose

Prologue: Pre-Constantinian Christian Movement, The True Flow of the Followers of Christ in the First Century

Believers in the messiah, Christ (Yahshua) were a mix of both Jews and Gentile followers. They were not Pharisaical legalists or Judaizers, but like their Savior worshipped the Creator in Spirit and in truth, with freedom. The Holy Spirit wrote the "love covenant" commandments on their hearts, producing the fruit of the Spirit from the tree of life.

They had "all authority in heaven and on earth" to make disciples and share the gospel to the whole world. Both Jew and Gentile were "one in the olive tree" of the true flow of Yahweh's covenants of blessing, that flowed from the righteous ones: Enoch, Able, Noah, Shem, Abraham, Isaac, Jacob (Israel), David and Yahshua. Gentile believers were grafted in, without having to become Jewish proselytes or cultural Jews. They were encouraged to walk in holiness, free from idolatry, and immorality.

Yahshua, the disciples/apostles, and the believers kept the true sabbath (Friday/Saturday), attended synagogues, kept the feasts, and on occasion, met for prayer, worship and teaching in various homes. They also gathered at the school of Tyrannus. Persecution drove them underground in caves and catacombs. Sometimes they met daily for the breaking of bread, communion, and prayer. Persecution came from both Hebraic legalists who rejected Yahshua as Messiah, and from Roman cruelty, whose gods would not allow worship of a god made flesh. Neither of these groups were a part of the true "olive tree" of covenant Israel.

Rome flowed out of Esau's loins, and was rooted in the Canaanite/Babylonian curse. Hebraic legalists developed a system of religious control through self-effort. They added to the Torah their own sets of rules and regulations.

Eventually, home meetings and public gatherings were called "Ecclesia" (where Koinonia took place) or the "called out ones." Research shows that the origins of the word "Church" refers to a building used for pagan worship, like worshipping the sun god.

Ecclesia is not the same as the Constantinian version of church/cathedral, which became like the Roman forum with a division between clergy and laity. These became huge wealthy structures, decorated in gold robbed from indigenous people.

Therefore, ecclesia is not a building, but simply a gathering together of true believers for prayer, worship, communion, and teaching.

Elders gave servant leadership and apostles planted these groups, and overseers coordinated various groups. Deacons gave practical service.

Leadership was from the bottom up. Many leaders had jobs and vocations. Paul was a tent maker for instance. These were like "little menorahs" or candlesticks in each location where "one another" ministry took place. They confessed their sins to one another, forgave one another, encouraged, and exhorted one another, and loved one another.

Prophesy, tongues, interpretation, words of wisdom and knowledge flowed by the gifts of the 7-fold Spirit in each menorah (Isaiah 11:1-5). The ecclesia was firmly rooted in the "olive tree" of the covenant of blessing flowing through Israel and the true Hebrew root system. This was in contrast to the later Constantinian church which had Babylonian pagan roots.

The believers in Yahshua as Messiah still celebrated "shabbat" and they embraced the integrative flow of both the first and second covenant scriptures. They held to the marriage love covenant of Israel to Yahweh expressed in the commandments, which were now fulfilled by Christ. His life, death, and resurrection restored us back into full intimacy with the Father. Yahshua was the second Adam. Believers could now walk and talk with Abba and eat from the tree of life, Yahshua.

      Synagogues were simply gathering places for traditional Jews to meet, break bread, and celebrate the Passover deliverance. They also pronounced blessings, did Torah teaching, and all in attendance could participate. However, many synagogues refused to acknowledge Yahshua as Messiah, and would not welcome believers. However, some became messianic and out of this the ecclesia, "the called-out ones," transitioned, yet still rooted in Hebraic roots. Gentiles were only required by the apostles to avoid eating meat offered to idols, strangled animal meat, drinking blood, and sexual immorality.

      Samaritans, who were half breed remnants of the ten tribes who were assimilated, also had a part in the ecclesia of believers. The woman at the well, not only evangelized her town, but became an apostle leader, according to church history.

The reason for writing this is, when the church of today comes out of its Babylonian pagan roots instituted by Constantine, the evil Catholic church, and the reformation of this Babylonian system, and then becomes a transformed ecclesia with an olive tree root system,... then what will the ecclesia really look like? I believe it will look like the first century ecclesia described in my writings here!

Unfortunately, the enemy stopped the flow of this ecclesia by creating a counterfeit perverted form of a reconstructed Christianity with pagan Babylonian roots, which operated very much like witchcraft, spreading evil throughout the world. An example of this was in the indigenous Native boarding schools. The Catholic church abused young tribal kids by rounding them up with gun boats, and then placing in pedophile rings for the pleasure of the priests. They also forcibly castrated many, and gifted them smallpox embedded blankets. They were stripped of their language, culture, regalia, and family ties. Many were murdered and placed in mass graves.

Also, in Boston, the Globe newspaper reported that 87 Catholic priests had abused up to 900 young boys and girls there. These priests were protected by the church who claimed to represent God. This was the same "Jesus" that they taught about to First Nation's peoples. No one in my culture wants that "Jesus." That's why we refer to Creator's Son by His real name "Yahshua" a tribal person, the great high chief of the lion tribe.

Transformation Of The Church
"Come Out Of Babylon"

Chapter One: The History Of The Reformed Church

    The Church has attempted to go through a reformation under Luther, Calvin, and many other reformers. Through them Catholic canonized scriptures have been translated and made available to all. However, what system were they trying to reform and improve on? The first pope and conqueror Constantine cut off all Jewish roots under the threat of death and removal, to those who worshiped on the Sabbath or who kept the feasts, etc. Then he replaced Jewish roots with a pagan form of reconstructed Christianity. This evil system became wealthy with greed and attempted to dominate all the kingdoms of the world. They slaughtered millions who attempted to translate the scriptures or even challenge their system. This took place through the inquisition, the crusades, and by conquering the New World. In the middle East, it was "kill a Muslim for Jesus." In Europe and England, it was by burning Bible translators at the stake. In the New World it was by slaughtering the welcoming indigenous Natives and robing their lands and gold. As previously stated, they rounded up Native children in my culture with gunboats and forceably placed them into assimilation boarding schools, where they were used for the pedophile pleasure of the priests, and many were castrated and given blankets embedded with smallpox. Their names, language, and family cultural ties were taken from them, and they were given a number. Hitler studied these schools. Many died and were buried in mass graves.

    The pagan roots that this new perverted form of Christianity, go back to Babylon and the Canaanite curse. <u>This is the root system of even today's contemporary Church.</u> When you draw nutrients and sustenance from a polluted root system, then try to reform a pagan system, you still end up with a polluted version of the original first century Church!

    Esau, who was cursed, became the progenitor of Edom, and eventually Greece and Rome. One would wonder why the church has made little change in the world today? The church is flowing out of a cursed Babylonian/Canaanite root system! An example of this was the removal of the "Olive Tree" (Romans chapter 11) that the church should be grafted into, from which would flow the blessing from Abraham, Isaac, Jacob, David and Yahshua. Anything rooted in Jewish roots were forbidden by the first Catholic councils. For instance, if Christians worshiped on the Sabbath, (Friday/Saturday), or celebrated the feasts, or kept the commandments, they were either killed or excommunicated to ghettos, or exiled to other countries. This is where the "Jewish problem" began. It is interesting to me that Yahshua (meaning Yahweh is salvation) was a Jew, the disciples were Jews, they worshiped on the Sabbath in Jewish synagogues, and they celebrated the feasts.

      Constantine then decided to change the date of the resurrection of Yahshua from the dead, to correspond with his worship of the goddess Ishtar, the queen of Babylon, where children were sacrificed to the god Moloch and their blood was used to dye eggs, to celebrate the spring solstice. Today the church celebrates "Ishtar" day or Easter, with special services and Easter egg hunts. The Eastern Orthodox church refused this, and separated from the Western papal rule and control. Then Constantine changed the day of worship from the Sabbath, to the day he worshiped his sun-god, on Sunday, because he saw a cross in the sun when defeating Rome. Christmas was instituted in the fourth century to celebrate the pagan holiday of

"Saturnus," where trickster rituals were done on each day portraying evil. Then came the sale of indulgences to raise more money, with the promise of buying a loved one out of purgatory. The saying was "a coin in the coffer rings, a soul from purgatory springs." This was the essence of the Canaanite curse. Cain means "to acquire" materialistically. A description of the satanic strategy in scripture is to gain control by trade, material gain, and dominating warfare. All greed flows from this curse.

      That is why Columbus slaughtered indigenous Natives in order to acquire gold for Queen Jezebel's (Isabella), cathedrals in Spain. The cathedrals were designed after the Roman forum, bringing a separation between the laity and the clergy. The monarchical episcopate set up a form of government opposite of Yahshua's principles of servanthood and humility. The church became rich with possessions and property. This is not a system that was exemplified by the giving modeled by the early church.

Finally, this perverted form of Christianity began changing the very names of Yahshua & Yahweh. Yahshua was Christ's real Jewish name, which has a strong sense of deity. It means, "Yahweh is salvation." A first century priest mispronounced it to "Yesu" and then to Jesus. Jesus can refer to any Greek god and does not have the same authoritative sense of deity. The word "God" came from the Germanic word "Gad" like gad fly, a sensual term. At least they were not Jewish sounding! Are you beginning to get the picture?

    Then on top of this the Constantinian church claimed to be the "New Israel." This would then replace completely the real "Olive Tree" of Israel. This was the beginning of what is known as "Replacement theology," which is everywhere in the church today.

Chapter Two: "Come Out Of Babylon"

Revelation chapter 18 rings out these end times warnings:
"After these things I saw another angel coming down out of heaven having great authority and the earth was filled with light from His glory...and he cried with a great voice saying Babylon the great has fallen and has become a dwelling place of those possessed by demons and a home for every foul spirit...the wine of the anger of her fornication which all nations and the kings of the earth have drunk by committing fornication with her, and the merchants of the earth have become rich from the power of her trade...I heard another voice out of heaven saying <u>come out of Babylon my people, that you may not share in her sins and not receive of her plagues!</u>"

This Babylonian system is a deeply rooted global system that will be judged by Yah in the last days. If we don't come out of this root system, then we will indeed be judged along with Babylon. This will open us up to receiving her plagues given by the death angel in the last days. Yahweh's wrath is coming on this evil root system for her luxurious and immoral lifestyle and its oppression on the world. This judgment not only results in disease and contagion, but also the collapse of world economies.

Later in this passage it talks about this system's deception of its followers through "pharmakia." and drugs, which is equated with sorcery.

Therefore, we as the church are exhorted to "come out of Babylon" and its church and global system. What is needed, is not a reformation of a paganized church, but rather a transformed, repentant church with a new root system firmly planted in the "Olive Tree" of our Hebraic root system of blessing. We should have been grafted into it by the death and work of our Messiah Yahshua, who is a tribal person. He is the great high chief of the lion tribe of Judah, a Jew!

This is not to say that we should embrace Hebraic Judaism of the pharisees/Sadducees and become a Jewish proselyte. I am also not suggesting that we become Judaizers. I am suggesting that we return to our true faith roots that were exemplified by our Hebraic covenant followers such as Abraham, Israel, David & Yahshua.

Even Yahshua couldn't swallow the old wine of the scribes, pharisees, and Sadducees, yet He incorporated the most ancient love covenant manifested by a complete fulfillment of the commandments written on our hearts. This was Yahweh's marriage covenant of love. Both the first and second covenant scriptures flow together to form a solid foundation and root system.

    The church needs to study the Hebraic historical context behind the written scriptures. I would suggest purchasing a copy of the" Tanach" and the "Chumash," with Hebrew commentaries. Also, a study of the Hebrew alphabet would help one gain new revelation, as each letter has deep spiritual insight.

    The new wine is the fulfilled Messianic completion of the first covenant. Also, it is the incorporation of both Jew and Gentile as one in the "Olive Tree." It is not a replacement system of pagan perversion rooted in the Babylonian root system!

    I am not convinced that the current "Messianic" form of Christianity totally does what is needed, however this movement does operate from the "Olive Tree" root system. I believe what is needed is a combined root system of both Judah and Joseph (ten tribes of Israel, assimilated into indigenous tribes).

    Therefore, we desperately need to come out of Babylon and reunite with our true Hebraic roots before we receive the same judgment that is promised to the Babylonian system by Yah (short for Yahweh, meaning judge).

Chapter Three: Two Sticks Become One

One of the earliest mission groups that represented truth to America were the Moravian missionaries. A group of them settled in Moravian Falls, NC. They had a vision for the uniting of Native Americans with Jewish believers. They buried a covenant to this effect in the earth at Moravian Falls. I was invited a year ago to come to Moravian Falls as a Native Mi'kmaq elder to do a small drum circle gathering. I anticipated maybe 12-15 people. The Messianic leader there also suggested doing a small powwow as well, because of the Native people in attendance. Then a last-minute thought came to us, to perhaps do a two-stick ceremony.

In Ezekiel chapter 37, there is written a prophesy that instructs the hearer to write the name Judah on one stick, for Judah and Benjamin, and to write the name Joseph on the other for the ten tribes of Ephraim which had been divided from Judah.

In the book "Out of the Flames" by James Adair, he was an anthropologist who lived and studied with North American indigenous tribes for 37-years in the 17th century. He studied both the language and the culture. He concluded that they had

Hebraic roots. Jonathan Edwards agreed. For instance, the Cherokee had cities of refuge, carried an ark into battle with them, celebrated lunar festivals, and sang drum chants to Yahweh. Their name for the Creator was "Yoh Hei Wah" or Jehovah. A group of my Native friends went to Jerusalem and were singing Native drum songs, and were approached by conservative Jews asking them how they knew these ancient Jewish songs? The Cherokee trace their roots back to Joseph in ancestral writings.

    To continue the story, I cut a large stick in half lengthwise, on one I wrote Judah, and the other Joseph. As a Native I carried the Joseph stick, and my Messianic friend Sion Rose carried the Judah stick. The Ezekiel prophesy describes the bringing together of the 2-sticks as one (echad) whole stick. This represented the bringing together of the divided nations of Israel back together as one nation restored again.

    So, because of the Moravian vision, we did a ceremony at the powwow and united Joseph and Judah back together as one. When we did this and tied them as one with blue and white ribbons, suddenly a strong wind blew, but not in the trees. Immediately, the 125 people who witnessed this spontaneously began leaping and praising Yahweh! Then 2-eagles flew across the East gate of the powwow circle in low formation like F-16s. I blew my eagle whistle. Earlier I danced the sacred eagle dance representing the Creator. Bells were heard. Later photography revealed the presence of 2-angels. It was unbelievable! We believe this was a sign of future Israel coming back together in the end of time. I also believe that this was a sign for the church to reunite with our Hebraic roots in the "Olive Tree" as we renounce our Babylonian roots.

    In the garden of Eden there were 2-trees. The tree of life, with 12-fruits represented Yahshua, the second Adam, who reunites us to this tree of life and blessing. I believe the 12-fruits are healing that flows from it, wisdom from above, eternal life and the 9-fruits of the Spirit.

    The other tree is the tree of mixture of good and evil, which flowed out through the curse of Cain and the Canaanites, and eventually the rebellion of the Rephaim Nimrod, who tried to assault the heavenly throne by building a star-gate on Babel's tower. This satanic system evolved into Babylon, the worship of Ishtar (Isis, Diana, Mary etc.) and Baal and Ashtaroth worship.

Today's church is full of mixture as we see the integration of holy yoga (inviting demons through various positions), mindfulness, Eastern meditations, false prophesies, demonic false laughter, and evangelists promising money returned if you give to their ministry and so on. No wonder, it flows out of the Babylonian root system and are the same evil roots from which the church draws its sustenance.

Chapter Four: Taking Off the Blinders

You say, "Oh but my church has wonderful worship and challenging messages. People who attend are well-dressed and live good lives. We stay separate from the evil world, and have a beautiful, comfortable facility. We are well-versed on theology and apologetics. We have a wonderful church, and great social interaction."

One must only look beyond the surface to see reality. Statics show that 3 out of 10 in the pews have life-controlling issues that they hide in secrecy and shame. You cannot talk openly about them because you must appear to have it "all together." These days contemporary worship has questionable theology in its lyrics, and often you are issued earplugs to mute the volume as you enter a dark night club setting. Guilt focused messages are preached to attempt to scare the devil out of you, raise more finances, or as a guilt trip to scare you into heaven. The truth is, Abba wants to welcome us back home into His heart of love.

Normally the church is not a place where sinners are welcomed, and there isn't a place at the table for people like LGBTQ strugglers, prostitutes, and street people.

We have rejected those, who Yahshua came to reach, by our false separation from the world. An example of this is Christ's encounters with the woman at the well, and with Mary Magdalene.

Having the proper theology and rational knowledge, many times excludes approaching the Creator in the Spirit. Yahshua taught worshiping in Spirit and truth. We need to follow what the Spirit says and does. Today the Bible is worshiped more than the "Living Word" Yahshua (John chapter 1).

Some churches are more like a social club. Gossip runs rampant, in place of deep intimate relationships. No longer do we meet to confess sins and shortcomings, to encourage, and to exhort one another in the atmosphere of unconditional love. Where are those who walk in close holiness and deep love and intimacy with Abba, and each other?

In the last days it has been prophesied that deceptions and a strong delusion would affect even the very elect. Let me attempt to wake you up out of your false matrix of reality, to see things as they really are. Answer these questions:

- Do you see money changing and wealth getting in the church today?

Example: One radio evangelist promised to send an autographed picture of Jesus for a $100 ministry gift.
- Do you see the celebration of pagan holidays through Easter egg hunts, etc. in the church?
- Are church members heavily medicated by the use of pharmakia?
- Are many in the church addicted to drugs and alcohol?
- Is sexual licentiousness a problem in the church?
- Can a person only be accepted in the church if they are a heterosexual struggling with sexual addiction, or other life-controlling issues?
- Do you see the presence of demonic affliction in those who have emotional problems in the church?
- Is there any tendency to dominate or control on the part of the clergy or church leadership?
- Do members react when pointing out the need for connecting with our Hebraic roots, the commandments, or the teachings on the feasts?
- How often do you hear the out of context verse, "We are not under law but under grace?"

Example: Ask yourself, which of the commandments would you eliminate as no longer valid?
- Have you ever had Torah teaching?
- Is there an anti-Semitic, anti-Jewish sentiment in your church?
- Are there members who basically want to ignore, or do away with what is commonly referred to as the "Old testament?"
- Does worship not take place on the true Sabbath (Friday/Saturday), where the Sabbath is honored and respected as Holy before Yahweh?

One time I was counseling a man like this, who also did not believe in the power and gifts of the Holy Spirit. I instructed him to bring a pair of scissors, as we were going to cut out of his Bible the parts he no longer believed to be relevant. As we attempted to do just that, he backed down and refused with embarrassment. This is basically what secessionists believe. They fail to see the unity of both the first and second covenants. Yahshua taught the first covenant scriptural truth and how the Torah spoke of His prophetic fulfillment, as He walked with believers on the road to Emmaus. He quoted about His fulfillment and ministry of salvation from Isaiah 61. Anytime it referred to scripture in the New Testament, it was referring to the first covenant scriptures, as the New testament had not yet been written. Yahshua was a Torah teacher who introduced the fulfillment and completion of its truth.

    If many answers to the above questions are" yes," perhaps it would be good to open your spiritual eyes and anoint them with eye salve that you might see.

Chapter Five: Get in The Flow

Trees and plants receive their nourishment from the absorption flow that comes up from the roots embedded in the soil. A bad root system produces deformed growth and eventual death. I had a friend who recently had a dream/vision about a large number of dead trees with overgrown roots. They had to be removed roots and all and be disposed of.

Yahshua taught about the vine and the branches, that unless one was abiding (connected to) in the right vine (Himself), it would not bring forth the good fruit (of the Spirit). Otherwise it would be cut off and burned in the fire. Today the axe is laid to the root, and it is time for trans-formative change.

Today the kingdom of Elohim is moving and flowing in the earth. His Spirit (Roark Ha Kodosh) is moving and flowing in many unusual ways, like the wind. In order to reach today's younger generation, the old wine of the organized church will not do the job. It is going to take the new wine of the flow of the Spirit to affect changes in this generation.

I go into places with the gospel that most church people will not go into. Because of Abba's love flowing through me, I go into

LGBTQ gatherings, with hugs of love and compassion. I share the good news that Abba wants to welcome them into His heart of love. My goal is to get Yahshua into their hearts and let Him do any changing from the inside out. I do the same with the Trans community. I share the benefits of reparative therapy for both heterosexual and homosexual past hurts. I attend healing circles where they do reiki laying on of hands, and end up bringing deliverance to them flowing out of love. I have attended Edgar Casey mindfulness meditation groups and do the same.

In Native circles I frequently encounter Wicca and witchcraft. I challenge them to come up to the 3rd heaven where the real power is, through the gatekeeper High Priest Yahshua. When they ask me to pray, I neutralize the demonic power in their Tarot cards. At least they are open to the supernatural realm, whereas most of the church does not believe or operate in the supernatural realm. This is sad as we have the real thing available to us through the work of the 2nd Adam, who restores us back to the garden, where we can walk and talk with Yahweh, see the angels, and eat from the tree of life. Most believers only access less than 20%

of what is available to them through the flow of the Spirit.

    Therefore, the "Wind" that is Holy" is blowing and flowing, but not through a Babylonian root system. There is a strong hydraulic flow of the Spirit available through holy channels that are set in the truth. Some time ago, I had a vision of the revival of a new form of worship, coming from indigenous Native people, that resulted in a tidal wave of revival and renewal. As it began to gather strength, churches rooted in the Babylonian root system were washed away and flooded. Those who were rightly rooted in the truth became like surfers riding on top of the wave and flowing with it. This wave flowed together with other tidal waves in different parts of the world.

    Very little can flow through a blocked pipe. Worse yet how would you feel if you turned on your kitchen faucet and slime came out? My challenge is to do whatever you need to do to get in the pure end time flow of the Spirit.

Chapter 6: How to Change Root Systems

The term Paul uses in Romans chapter 11, is "grafted in." A branch needs to be cut off from, in this case the Gentile tree, releasing it from its root system, and become an integral part of the Jewish root system through the "Olive Tree." The graft needs to be matched in a way that the veins and rings of the mother tree lines up with the grafted-in branch, so that it receives the very essence and substance of the roots of the "Olive Tree," and that they flow together as one.

The true root flows from Yahweh, through the righteous ones (Enoch, Melchizedek, Elijah, etc.) and then through the Abrahamic covenant, through Israel (Jacob), the Davidic covenant (root of Jesse), down through Yahshua. Matthew 1:1 states, "Christ, the son of Abraham, and the son of David."

The "Olive Tree" roots do not flow through Hebraic phariseeism or the Judaizer spirit, which were set in opposition to the ministry of Yahshua and the disciples. However, it does flow through Yahweh's marriage covenant to Israel when they came out of Egypt. This covenant of love was written in the commandments.

They are summarized by loving Yahweh with all your heart, soul, strength, and mind, and loving your neighbor as yourself. Christ stated that He came not to do away with the law, but to complete and fulfill it. His love was expressed through the "Living Water" that He gave to the woman at the well. She was an inferior woman; a half breed Jew and had tried finding satisfaction through six men. She became the first person that Yahshua revealed that He was the Messiah to! After receiving the "Living Water" of His love, she not only won over her village, but historically became an Apostle in the early church.

Let me ask you this? What kind of bridegroom would establish His marriage covenant vows, and then turn around and say that because of His grace, it's fine with Him if you involve yourself in adultery, satanism or sorcery? He is a covenant keeping God! Would you want your partner to live under the grace of doing whatever their flesh wanted to do?

Lastly, we see taught in Romans chapter 11, that the reason we have been grafted in, is to provoke Israel to jealousy. How can we provoke them to jealousy if we do not worship on Shabbat, or we refuse to avail ourselves of the option of keeping or knowing about the feasts? How can we provoke to jealousy when we have little knowledge of Jewish culture and practices? Do we even know the "Shema" or how to pray a Hebrew blessing?

Have we studied the Hebrew alphabet and learned the pictorial, musical, and numerical meaning of each letter? You can preach a message on each one. "Glory of Zion" ministries of Texas (Chuck Pierce) has many good books and resources on this. Do we know the 365 names of God in scripture? Each name has a number, musical notes, and a specific meaning. I believe that in heaven, He will reveal more about who He really is through His names. Have you ever studied Hebrew history and commentaries? My chief Suuqiina is a Hebrew scholar and has written a book on this. He leads a powerful indigenous ministry called, "Indigenous Messengers International."

So then how can we provoke Israel to jealousy? I was at the airport one day and saw a Jewish man in regalia, who wore stringed zit zits hanging from his belt. Each knot represents the names of Yahweh. For instance, the woman with the issue of blood actually grabbed Yahshua's zit zits to receive her healing.

So, I sat next to the man and grabbed his zit zits and said what traditional Jews would say, "teach me your faith."
We talked for about an hour and afterward he stated that I had actually taught him. I had shared about my indigenous Hebraic roots that were expressed in my Native culture and drum chants. I believe that I had indeed provoked him to jealousy, as I shared about my Messiah Yahshua. I do a lot of studying expressed in the original languages of the Scriptures. I do not claim to be a messianic Christian, but rather a Native American with Hebraic roots. My chief has taught me a lot about our culture. My heart is to see the church fully transformed as it aligns itself with the root system that will flow out renewal and blessing! AHO!

BONUS BOOK

What's Wrong With The Church?

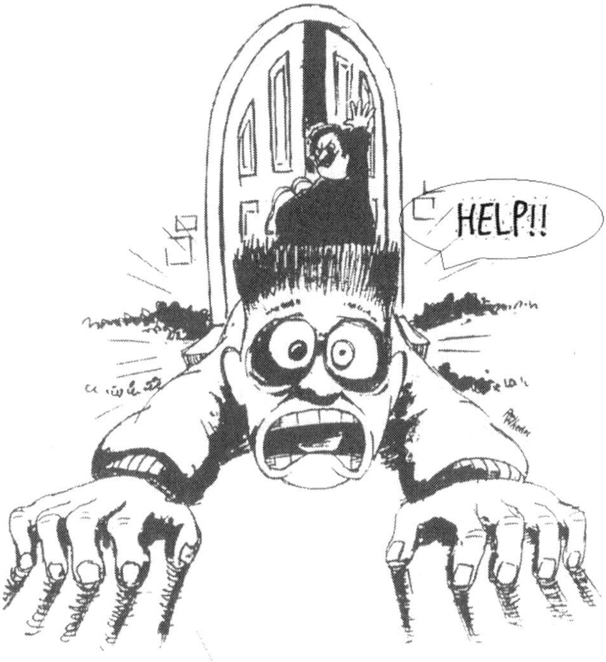
HELP!!

Chapter 1
WESTERN WORLD VIEW

The roots of Christianity were based primarily on a Hebrew world view. Later through the conquering of Alexander the Great, the Hebrew culture was overlaid with a Greek mind-set. Eventually, a Roman overlay came in on top to bring in a more Western world view.

The Hebrew world view had the Creator integrating with His creation which manifested a message of who Yahweh was through His creation (Psalm 19, Romans 1:20). All things expressed His presence and life. Our role here was to be caretakers of creation, and not to exploit it, or rape its resources. It was not His desire that we destroy our life support system through pollution. Certainly sending His Son Yahshua our Messiah, was a clear example of Yahweh's integration and involvement in our lives through redemption. Yahshua showed us who the Father really was, and demonstrated His love (Heb 1:3). Therefore, one should approach and worship Yahweh in the spirit supernaturally (John 4:23).

However, the Greek/Roman world view had more of a Canaanite/Babylonian influence which was dualistic in nature. It was based on trying to connect with the "Life-Force" in the universe by worshipping parts of it, and included idolatry. Power, control, and material gain over other people would somehow connect one with this universal "Life Force." The Gnostics of Greece for instance, separated the natural/physical world from the supernatural realm. They couldn't process how a Creator could be made flesh and dwell among us (John 1:14). They concluded that Yahshua was just a disembodied spirit. Add to this the Roman view of the age of reason and the scientific approach. Here one could only connect with God or the gods, by a logical systematic theology and apologetics. No longer did believers need to approach God in the Spirit.

    Up until the first century, the church maintained its Hebrew roots and world view. After Constantine conquered Rome, he went about creating his own version of Christianity, stripping it of all Hebrew roots. He then integrated his paganistic beliefs into this new version of Christianity, which has continued even today through our reformed churches.

    For instance, his first council forbade, under threat of death, the worshipping on the Sabbath, or keeping any of the Hebrew feasts and celebrations. He changed the day of worship to coincide with his worship of the sun god on Sunday (He saw the cross in the sun) . Then he decided to go against the date of resurrection day, rightfully celebrated by the Eastern Orthodox church, to the day he worshipped Ishtar queen of Babylon (Baal/Ashtoreth), where the sacrifice of children to Moloch took place, using their blood to dye eggs. Therefore, today the church celebrates Ishtar day (Easter) where we have kids hunt for Easter eggs. The worship of Ishtar gave rise to Isis of Egypt, Diana of the Ephesians, and the worship of Mary the Queen of heaven. Basically, it is the mother/child cult that has enslaved 1/3 of the world's population.

      If that wasn't bad enough, he then began persecuting Jews, and exporting them out of Europe. He only wanted the Western world view to dominate this new form of Christianity. As the result we have a church polluted with a pagan Greek/Roman distortion of Christianity. Up until Constantine, the church was firmly set in a Hebrew world view and root system (Romans 11:11-24). Yahshua was a Jew, the disciples were Jews, and the church leaders were Jewish. Gentile believers were grafted in to the main trunk of Israel.

Constantine then fostered a world dominating religion, which controlled Kings, Nations and lands through the doctrine of "Manifest Destiny." The savage inquisition, the crusades and the raping of gold resources for the church followed.

Then came the persecution of Bible translators by burning them at the stake. This led to "killing a Muslim for Jesus" crusades to conquer the Holy land. They thought by bringing back pieces of the cross, and other relics to Rome, this would bring special powers. Eventually this led to the murderous Inquisition. Then the church expanded into the new world and rounded up indigenous children away from their families with gun boats, placing them in boarding schools. Their goal was to strip them of their culture and identities, and to persecute them through pedophilia, small pox blankets, and outright murder. Then they proceeded to take control of their lands for the Church. No wonder the priests dress in black!

Even though the Church went through a reformation, much of the pagan roots and Western world view was imbedded in this distorted form of Christianity. It flowed from the "Tree of Mixture (Good/evil)." It now has an outward form of religion and goodness, but is far from the teachings of Yahshua. Today three out of ten in our Churches have life controlling issues, according to statistics, yet none feel free to expose them to others in the Church. We have an ideal surface form of Christianity, where the people in the pews hide in secrecy. In the early Church they met to confess faults to each other, pray for one another, exhort one another, encourage one another, and love one another. Today there's no room at the table for someone struggling with sexual addiction, pornography, homosexuality, addiction, or infidelity. Most try to look good, and appear good. It's mostly a social club where we go to feed our minds with "right doctrine", but not to change our lives or to live in spiritual intimacy with the Father.

    The Hebrew world view leads one to manifest and integrate the indwelling of the Father in every aspect of our lives. He desires to fully live in us, in every part of our lives, and that we would live in Him fully.

    John chapter one explains that Yahshua was in the very bosom of the Father's love, and then He became flesh and habitated with us to show us what the Father was like. The Tabernacle in the wilderness and the feast of

Tabernacles showed us that the Father desired to be presence with us in our daily lives. In the garden of Eden, He walked and talked with Adam. The second Adam Christ has restored us to this spiritual intimacy. However, in our Christianity today many are hanging in to live the "Nasty now-and-now", and are waiting for the "Great by-and-by" in the sky to connect with God. Yahshua (Hebrew name for Jesus) taught that the kingdom of heaven is accessible, it's in you, and all around you. In Him we live and move and have our being, Paul taught. Therefore, it's this separation of the dichotomous Greek/Roman world view, taught in Gnosticism, that has kept us distant from Yahweh (Hebrew name for God), and His supernatural power in changing our lives. Today most Christians don't even believe in the supernatural. This is sad!

    In order to unwrap the choke hold of the Greek/Roman world view on the Church, we need to explore its roots. We can trace its roots back to the "Tree of mixture" and the "Canaanite curse." I previously mentioned this curse connected with the Babylonian system. In Revelation it teaches believers to "Come out of her." (Rev 18:4)

Cain means "to acquire." Cain murdered his brother Able. Murder, city building and the curse followed his generations. Cain tried to obtain favor by the fruit of the earth. His seed passed down through Noah and his wife who were descendants of Cain, and then through the curse of Ham, the exposer of nakedness. Through his generations came Nimrod who founded Babylon, and built a tower to try to assault the throne of God. Also, he fathered Canaan and eventually the philistines. When Abraham came into the promise land, he was at odds with the Canaanites. What was there about these cursed descendants that was an abomination to God?

Chapter 2
THE CANAANITE CURSE

The descendants of Cain began worshipping the creation, the "Life force" in the universe and were given to idolatry, instead of worshipping Yahweh. Their focus was on fertility, seed, wealth, power and control.

It's interesting to note here, that this was the doctrine of the fallen cherub Lucifer in Ezekiel 28. When one studies this passage there is a focus on material gain of wealth, self-glorification, pride, rebellion, mixing of good and evil, and becoming your own god. From this flows the Babylonian system of Baal/Ashtoreth, Ishtar the Queen of heaven, Isis of Egypt and the mother/child cult, even in the Catholic Church where Mary is deified. Out of this flowed witchcraft, sorcery, and ruling people with cruelty, also national conflicts. This is all part of the wisdom that is from below (James 3).

In contrast to this satanic system, is what flowed out of the "Tree of life." This tree is personified by Yahshua, and produces the fruit of the spirit, wisdom from above, holiness, and intimacy with the Lord. Healing, forgiveness and love also flow from the healing streams of this tree, which also appears at the end of Revelation.

Now we get to the interesting aspects of the Canaanite curse. Again, the goal was to connect with the "Life force" of nature by acquiring power, wealth, control and dominance. Power came by dominating other people and nations, and their life was contained in the blood. Fertility was obtained by sowing seed. By the time it appeared in Sodom, if a stranger wandered in, married men would sodomize him to plant the seed of life, then they would murder him, drink his blood now fertilized, and eat his flesh. This would give the gift of virility and power in order to connect with the "Life force," and also to control others. This was the abomination in Sodom.

This is in a different world from the gay community today with those who have monogamous same sex relationships. By the time the Canaanite curse appeared in the New Testament, Paul spoke out against this abomination as it continued in the Greek culture. Here, married men would sodomize a young castrated boy in order to gain this same sense of power and virility. It was a practice in fertility ceremonies to integrate sexualization, in order to bless the seed and connect with the "Life force."

From this abomination, came human sacrifice, offering up children to Moloch, murder, wars, and international conflicts. It was through self-effort one obtained this force of nature, which led to separation and dualism, which flowed into the Western mindset.

These depraved people failed to understand that Yahweh was the complete source of life. One only needed to connect with Him to discover the value and dignity of human life. Within this is the love of the Father, forgiveness, reconciliation, and healing that are available to all.

In the Native indigenous world, this appeared by the human sacrifice system of the Mayans and the snake people.
By offering up human sacrifice, somehow this would ensure protection from the gods, fertility and appeasement of the life-force of nature.

There are ancient indigenous records of the appearance of a "Healer/Prophet/God/man" who was born of a virgin and was from a faraway land. He appeared to tribes all the way from Peru to Canada, and even in the pacific Islands. He did away with abuse, the snake people, human sacrifice and restored cultures and cities back to dignity and honor. These cities flourished under His leadership, and the Turtle people began to carry His message. The first people in America were the Lene Lenape who were Turtle people, who later became the Delaware tribe. In Canada He appeared to the 5-nations who were at odds with each other, as the "Peacemaker." These 5 (now 6) nations were at war with each other, abused their wives and children, and were going downhill fast. The Peacemaker took one arrow and easily broke it. Then He asked for 5 arrows which bundled together couldn't be broken. He brought unification of these 5-tribes, now 6, and the oldest unification agreement was birthed written in wampum, and is known today as the Iroquois covenant. Benjamin Franklin studied this covenant and formed our constitution on these principles. Our seal contains these arrows. Truly this was the "Prince of peace!"

    I believe most indigenous tribes have Hebrew roots. James Adair in his anthropological studies in the 17th century also concluded this, after living and researching Native cultures and languages, in his book, "Out of the flames." For instance, the Cherokee had cities of refuge, a priesthood, lunar festivals, carried an ark into battle, and had a worship center similar to the one in Jerusalem. They trace their roots back through Joseph who married the Egyptian daughter (dark skinned) of Potiphar.

    When Native drum song are chanted, often one hears "Yahweh" "Yo-Hei-Yah (Jehovah)," "Hei (Spirit)" and "Yah." A group of my indigenous friends went to Jerusalem and were playing Native drum chants by the gates, and Hasidic Jews approached them and asked how they knew these ancient Hebrew songs? I believe that indigenous tribes originated from the lost 10-tribes of Israel that were dispersed throughout the world. Yahshua, therefore came not only for Judah and Benjamin who returned intact from the Babylon captivity to Jerusalem, but for all of Israel. I believe these appearances occurred during the 40-days Yahshua rose from the dead before His ascension. Although Judah and Benjamin refused to receive Him as Messiah, the 6-nations did receive Him and are extending peace out to other nations.

    On a mission trip to the "World indigenous gathering" in South America, I was a part of a group that carried the wampum of the Iroquois which extend their peace covenant to the president of that country, who was indigenous. His representative received this with the 6-nations flag. I believe world peace will come through indigenous people, and not the politicians. We stand for a world view that is more consistent with the Biblical/Hebraic world view. The Greek/Roman dualistic world view that flows from the tree of mixture, and the Canaanite curse, has only resulted in wars, wealth hoarding, power and control, which has led to the destruction of our life support system with pollution, and environmental destruction through the raping of earth's resources.

    The 7th fire prophesy of many indigenous tribes states that a day is coming when the western world will disintegrate and self-destruct, and at that time they will look to indigenous people to teach them how to survive and care for our mother the earth. Aho!

Chapter 3
No Belief In The Supernatural

One of the effects of the Greek/Roman world view is a focus on the scientific/rational approach to theological studies. The "Age of reason" came to the church following the "Dark ages" and an avenue for defining God (Origin from the German word "gad," a sensuous term) flowed out of Greek logic. So great proofs were given for the existence of God, such as the ontological and teleological methods. One attempted to convince others through mental hypothesis and arguments. Today we see this in the teachings of systematic theology and apologetics. Somehow, we tried to approach the Creator through the mind. This fails to really connect one in an intimate way with Yahweh.

This is like trying to build a tower of logic, like Babel, to God, through "Correct doctrine", knowledge, and theological prowess. Knowledge and study of the scripture are assumed to be the vehicle to change our lives. Yet 3 out of 10 sitting in the pews have life controlling problems that are hidden, that knowledge doesn't even touch. True transformation comes only through the

Spirit of Yahweh, and the power of Yahshua! We need to worship and approach the Creator in spirit and in truth. It's not by our might but by His Spirit that transformation comes!

The Hebrew and Native world views have us to approach the Creator by the Spirit. Here we see the reality of the supernatural realm as it integrates into our everyday world through His kingdom on earth as it is in heaven. It's sad to say, but most Christians don't really believe in the supernatural world as it relates to everyday life. Our Native church takes place in the sweat lodge (no drugs, etc.) where we live in the supernatural world. Visions and dreams are common. One only needs to read the book of Acts to see the same things.

Somehow, we've been sold a bunch of lies that all the spiritual power gifts ended when the Catholic church canonized scripture. One only has to read church history to see that they continued in the early church ("Power Evangelism" by John Wimber). These so-called theologians also isogete I Corinthians 13 instead of exegeting the text properly. Spiritual power gifts will only end when we are with our Savior in heaven, and see Him "Face-to face."

In the passion translation from the

Aramaic, Yahshua says, "The kingdom of heaven is accessible to all.." We don't have to wait for the "Great by-and-by" to experience the supernatural realm, it's available now!

Let me tell you about my transformation in this regard. In college I was big into apologetics and studied Vantil and E.J.Carnell, and later Josh McDowell. I loved to debate and argue my point, it was a matter of pride. Then I became a missionary to Indonesia with the Navigators. Later I attended Denver seminary. After graduation, one of my goals was to straighten out charismatic's and Pentecostals. I had all the theological training and Biblical scripture to try to do so. I was very boring as a person.

I was a Christian counselor, and one day a Pentecostal woman handed me a box of tapes by John Wimber containing his "Signs and wonders" class at Fuller seminary. These tapes opened me up to desiring more of the release of the Spirit, which was in me, to fuller life and experience. Paul taught that he wanted to really "Know Christ" by experience (Gnosko) and the power of His resurrection. So, I asked the Lord to prepare my heart by seeking more of Him.

After listening to all these tapes which were oriented to my theology, this woman came by to collect them. I asked her to pray for me. She proceeded to lay hands on me and prayed powerfully. She then left me alone. What happened next was amazing. I fully describe it in another book I wrote.

To sum it up, I spent 3-hours on my face on the floor and was transformed into a mush-bucket baby. I laughed, I cried, I babbled in a baby language, and felt like I was more born again than my salvation confession years earlier. My spirit came to life, and I felt like I had entered into a new spiritual dimension. Next thing I knew, I was in the heavenlies sitting on "ABBA'S" lap. He said that He knew my alcoholic father had rejected me, but that He was my original Father, and He was going to take me up (Psalms 27:10). I literally felt His arms around me. He then commissioned me to speak in churches on unity. I told Him that I don't speak in churches, nevertheless within 2-weeks I had 6-speaking engagements in churches, where before that I had none. When I gave an invitation and prayed for people, stuff started happening. People got filled with the Spirit and delivered from evil spirits.

Next thing I knew, it was like living in the Book of Acts. Yahweh would wake me up to pray for people, and one night I had a vision of 2-kids in a fire. I interceded for them, and the next morning the headlines read, "Two kids luckily escape a gas explosion." I found out where they lived in a crack cocaine ghetto, and one grandmother told me she heard an audible voice from God saying "Get out now!" They were spared. The other grandmother heard an inaudible voice and got out in time. I had a chance to lead one of these boys to Christ, and bring them food and clothing. I've written another book describing similar miracles that exploded out of my life since my encounter with "ABBA."

One of the best things that happened was that God downloaded His love into me! It was like a substance that filled me up, and I've never been able to get over it! It has become the life force in my life that keeps me walking a holy walk today. (See my Facebook e-books)

Therefore, I went through the transition from a rational/mind-based Christianity, to living fully in the Spirit.

One of the first things I noticed, was that scripture exploded as I read it daily. Suddenly, I knew what it was like to follow after the Holy Spirit. What I read, I was experiencing in my own life. It was no longer theory, but practice and reality in everyday life. Beyond the sacred word, I saw the Lord!

He became the "Living Word" (John 1).

I also noticed that my prayer life had risen to a new dimension. It was not simply asking God for things, and that His will would be done, rather it became a forum for intimacy and praise. I began wanting to pray His prayers rather than mine. "What's on your mind and heart," I would ask? Revelation came after seeking Him, and I began declaring things He'd revealed. I prayed more by His faith in me, rather than my faith. "Have the faith that God gives, then you will say (Not pray) to that mountain, be thou removed and cast into the sea, and it shall be done." (Mark 11:22 and 23). It was unbelievable what took place after that.

My ministry took on a whole new focus as well. Prior to this I knew how to organize and crank out the ministry. I had been a student of church growth principles, and had led ministries both in the USA and in Indonesia. I was trained on how to make disciples and disciple-makers, who theoretically would multiply. Something was missing..."I" was doing the ministry, and not God. I even had success on the surface.

After my encounter with "ABBA," I started asking Him what He wanted to do and say. I was amazed after surrendering to what

He told me to do and say, powerful things began happening. I let Him totally control the meetings. People began getting healed and delivered. I opened the group to what others were sensing from God and a great oneness would fill the room. I thought to myself, "Duh! It seems like I would have let God minister earlier in life, rather than expend all the energy trying to do it myself!"

Chapter 4
The State Of The Local Church Today

I believe that the church today has gone from being a powerful movement, to being a sort of monument to Christianity. Young people aren't finding life and relevance in the local church, for what they are encountering in our culture today. Many are seeking spiritual reality in other venues. Some of these are in magic, the healing arts, the new age, Wicca, and even in drugs and witchcraft. Just take a poll of hands in your congregation as to who are Harry Potter fans? This is witchcraft 101. Basically, they are looking for the reality of the supernatural life in the church, and not finding it there! This is a travesty! We should be leading in this field, yet most believers, sadly, do not even believe in the supernatural realm.

The church has become a cozy, comfortable place of safety behind its closed walls, where most Christians hide from the everyday world. When a young person brings in a friend who is struggling with homosexuality, sexual addiction, pornography, drugs or alcohol, there is no room at the table. False images of superficial perfection must be maintained in our comfortable, cozy fellowships. Yet, as I have stated, statistics show that 3 out of 10 in the pew struggle with life controlling issues in secret, which gives fuel to the enemy.

Yahshua ministered to the lost sheep, to the outcasts and sinners, drunkards, and prostitutes. He declared that prostitutes would get into the kingdom before the religious leaders. The early church gathered to confess their faults, pray for one another, love one another, encourage one another, and exhort one another. Somehow, we've gotten off track. Yahshua taught that it was the sick that needed healing, and not those who considered themselves whole.

Also, the church has more of a focus on Biblical scholarship, than on doing the word, and in outreach into our cultural community. I get into places most believers don't even want to go. The other day, I went to a church for homeless street people and prostitutes. It was there I saw Jesus. On Palm Sunday they used tree branches instead of palms. There I sat with outcasts and sinners, listening to a prostitute pray. Worship took place, and food was distributed. They are also attacking social injustice issues by building tiny houses for the homeless.

  I am constantly challenging people to come up higher to where the real power and authority comes through Yahshua, who gives direct access into the supernatural realm as our High Priest.
  I been on the board of the LGBTQ elders through my work, and am close friends with the head of Blue Ridge gay pride in Asheville, NC. I'm also friends with the woman who wrote the Webster's dictionary definition of Transgendered, who is an international leader in the LGBT movement. I share the love of Abba, and the gospel of Christ. My goal is to get Christ inside of their lives, and let Him change what He wants from the inside out. Using this approach I believe we can really take the land for the kingdom. I actually do "Risk Prevention" seminars to help protect the young and vulnerable in these communities. In some cases, one out of five try suicide to escape the pressure. Where is the church?
  We have the Father's love, all authority in heaven and on earth, power from above, and should be filled with the Holy Spirit. The harvest is out there waiting to be reaped, yet we hide behind our church walls. Most of those I minister to have been hurt by their churches' rejection and religious spirit.

Something is not right!

Chapter 5
Hearing God's Voice

As I have stated, the first century church integrated paganism into the newly formed version of Christianity under Constantine, the first Pope. Then came the reformation under Luther, Zwingli, Calvin and other reformers who exposed the teachings of scripture. Biblical texts began to be printed, and no longer were they hidden by the scholars and priests to interpret. The Catholic church feared that if everyone interpreted scripture, they there would be many divisions and denominations. Sure enough, many different groups and types of churches emerged from the dark ages. You had Calvinistic, Armenian, free-will and Spirit-led divisions to mention a few. Yet they were all still infected by the paganized roots of the church they tried to reform.

Reformation really did not do the job! What was needed was "transformation." A return to first century Hebrew based Christianity. I am not referring to the "Judaizes" who opposed the gospel for a return to the proselyte system. I'm talking about a Hebraic Christianity that Cornelius experienced for instance. Christ said He came to fulfill the law, and the sending of His Spirit produced the fruit of the Spirit from the inside out. We are not under the religious oppression of the law, but the law is now written in our hearts. I'm also not talking about Messianic Christianity, but a pure integration of our Hebrew roots flowing into the life and teachings of Christ. For instance, there is a richness in worshipping on the Sabbath (Like the Adventist do) and celebrating the feasts as an option. They all point to our Savior.

    Finally, it would be valuable for the church to adopt the Hebrew world view. Yahweh desires to integrate with us by sending Immanuel to demonstrate who He really is. God desires to be with us and for us. He is not distant!

    With that in mind let's talk about His desire to talk with us every day, in a real and tangible way. In the garden, He walked and talked with Adam every day. This was lost by sin, but now regained by the second Adam Yahshua. I don't really think that most believers know what our potential is for spiritual intimacy made available by the work of the cross. Selah!

So, how do we hear the clear voice of God in our everyday lives? First it takes a listening spiritual ear, as you practice intimate worship in His presence. I highly recommend playing a soaking worship CD softly in the background. Julie True's soaking worship is my favorite (julietrue.com). As you relax and let stress go, let your focus be on Christ and His word. Tell Him about your love for Him and let your spirit worship.

Now different people have different ways of processing information. The Holy Spirit will use the way that is strongest for you. Some people are visual processors, and visual slides will mentally appear before your spiritual eyes. I am a visual processor and I often have very clear visions, which have future relevance. Others are verbal processors, and have scriptural downloads, or have words of knowledge, a specific "Rhema" word for them or others. Still others are kinesthetic processors and have a deep inner sense of God's presence or spiritual reality. They feel it deep inside their spirit. They just know when something isn't right.

So, while you're soaking in His presence, tune in to the way the Spirit is speaking to you individually. When you begin hearing that still small voice of the Lord, write it down for future reference. "Your ear shall hear a voice behind you saying, this is the way, walk ye in it..." Isaiah 30:21 "I will instruct you in the way you should go, I will give you good advice..." Psalms 32:8 and 9. Then it warns us not to be like a stubborn mule and resist. He wants to walk and talk with us! Aho!

ABOUT THE AUTHOR

Dan'El Garvin is a member of a North American people inhabiting the Maritime Provinces of Canada known as the Mi'kmaq. He is a Writer, Poet, Author, Missionary, Native American, Counselor, Eagle Dancer, Blowgun Champion and Conference Speaker. He has ministered and counseled all over North & South America and Indonesia.

His books are available in e-book form at Wayoftheraven.net/Destin-E Books under spiritual and non-fiction categories.

Websites:
Facebook at https://bit.ly/DanielGarvinFacebook
YouTube at https://bit.ly/DanielGarvinYouTube
E-Mail at agapedan1@aol.com

Dani'El Garvin
Two Native names
Okinow: "Bringer of light and life"
"E Gi Doh" Cherokee

- Mi'kmaq tribal elder and chief (Recognized in Trinidad and Land of Two Sands)
- Adopted into the Cherokee by clan mother and Snowbird elder (Via vision quest)
- Taught the Cherokee youth 3-years their culture (Flute, drum, dance, blow-dart, crafts)
- Pow wow competitive dancer including the sacred "Eagle dance"
- Pow wow arena director 4-years
- Acknowledged tribal medicine chief
- Attended world indigenous gatherings in South America and Trinidad
- Ministered prophetically to local tribes in jungle with native flute
- Acknowledged as chief in Trinidad during sacred ceremonies
- Featured in newspapers and on TV
- Lived on 6-nation's reserve on Grand river Canada, did ceremony there
- Ordained by "Indigenous Messengers International"

- Has performed Native weddings with drum and flute
- Cherokee blow-dart champion 5-years
- Reconciliation work to unite 2-cherokee tribes in SC
- Apart of the forgiveness movement in Canada to bring reconciliation and healing between Western boarding school abuse and Aboriginal people
- Skilled with medicine drum chants and Native flute
- Hosted many Native American gatherings
- Authored a book on First Peoples as well as has written many articles
- Taught Native American spirituality course, and led educational demonstrations in local libraries and museums